The Healing Goddess Oracle

Laurie Szott-Rogers

Circe Invidiosa
painted in 1892 by John William Waterhouse

The information presented within this book has been carefully researched and checked for factual accuracy. Nonetheless, the author and publisher make no warrantee; either express or implied, that the information contained herein is appropriate to every individual, situation and purpose, and assume no responsibility for errors or omissions. The reader assumes the risk and full responsibility for his or her actions, and the author and publisher will not be held responsible for any loss or damage, whether such loss or damage be consequential, incidental, special or otherwise, that may result from the information presented in this book.

The author has relied upon many sources, and her own experience, in compiling this book and has done her very best to check facts and to give credit where credit is due. Should any of the material contained in this book be inaccurate, or have been used without the proper permissions, please contact the author so that any oversight may be corrected.

ISBN 978-1-4959-6153-3

Published by - Prairie Deva Press

Gaia - An original photo illustration by Elena Ray.

Dedication

I would like to dedicate this book to my husband, Robert Rogers, my own personal Pan. He is a wonderful support and great inspiration to me. I am blessed with my mother Olga Szott, who is so dear to me.

Don Saunders is my design wizard, technical advisor and partner in creating. His input and talent manifests my dreams.

I am grateful for the talents and kindness of Paula Pesonen, Jo Ann Hammond-Meiers, Kenzie Volkov and Greg Clark who allowed me to use their beautiful art on my cards.

I have been reading cards with Janice Shoults and Paulette Grasley, for over 30 years. They are always in my heart.

My valuable friend, Dr. Devon Mark is an irreplaceable and encouraging spirit in my life. Dr. Jo Ann Hammond-Meiers, my friend, mentor and co-creator sparks and nourishes my life and projects.

Thanks also to my students, at Northern Star College, and my wonderful colleagues Catherine Potter, Skye MacLachlan, Jonathan Hooton and Nicole Martin.

Clarissa Pinkola Este's teachings have made an imprint on my soul, and her words come through on some of the oracles, especially Baba Yaga, Hades and Hekate. Stephen Aizenstat has also been a wonderful influence and his teachings are used when I talk about "breathing life into the tarot images". Thank you to the goddesses, gods and mythical images that enhance and enliven our life.

Enjoy the deck and the tarot. Let your own intuition guide your readings.

Gaia - From original photo illustrations by Elena Ray and Bluecrayola.

Pan - An original painting by Kuco.

Introduction

I have loved tarot, ever since Bob McDevitt introduced me to the Rider Deck, at age 13. The mesmerizing characters and the bright colors made my sense of wonder rise, as I glimpsed into future possibilities through symbols. I bought many sets of tarot after that and was always delighted by the imagery and sense of possibility the decks evoked. I found the Mother Peace when I was in my mid twenties and as I flipped through the cards and write ups of the goddess, I knew the story being told was one of a deeper, older truth, than my history books had revealed.

I have been a teacher of metaphysics and alternative therapies for over 25 years. The goddess keeps coming back to me in many ways and forms. I have had the privilege of teaching courses, writing books and making aromatic blends, all highlighting her many aspects.

This deck however, is comprised of gods goddesses and mythical beings. Each of these guides brings insights, blessings and meaning. They represent thousands of years of tradition and collective unconscious patterns.

Using The Healing Goddess Oracle cards helps us find out 'who is showing up', on that day, week or year of our lives and tap into what their message might be.

Attuning to which archetypal teacher is present makes life lessons easier and more fun.

In this deck, the Gods and Goddesses are not paired with the Tarot figures in a conventional manner. Yet, each of the beings adds some new energy and perspective to traditional placements. Greek Gods and Goddesses represent the major arcana, in the first 22 cards.

There are some alterations to the names of the classical major arcana, as the Celestial teachers bring in a slightly different energy- for example, Death is renamed the Crossroads, Judgment is referred to as Wise Response.

The remainder of the oracle cards (non-major arcana) represents deities from diverse traditions, plus a couple of magical teachers, that are not technically Gods or Goddesses. Instead of using the classical minor arcana, Shamans, Mavens and Magi inhabit this deck. The common suits of cups, swords, wands and pentacles, date back to an even older origin. The four elements, where all life comes from preceded the suits. Water represents cups and emotion, earth carries the abundant and material, pentacle energy, air is equivalent to swords and the intellect and fire like wands, is a suit of spirit.

The Shamans represent the first level of accomplishment. The Mavens and Magi are both masters of the elements and skills they represent. The deck has 34 cards in total. Please use your own intuition and insight to add to what each of the Gods or Goddesses is saying to you, when you consult the oracle.

Oracle Cards

Your purchase of this book licenses you to download a free set of printable oracle cards for your personal use. For instructions on how to obtain this beautiful set of cards, please see page 41.

Layouts and Spreads

There are a plethora of wonderful spreads possible. I will suggest a few that I have found most accessible. If you have other spreads you prefer, use them.

The One Card Draw

Ask a question and draw a card to give insight around the answer.

The 3 Card Draw

The first card represents past events, the second is the present moment and the third gives context about the future.

The Celtic Cross:

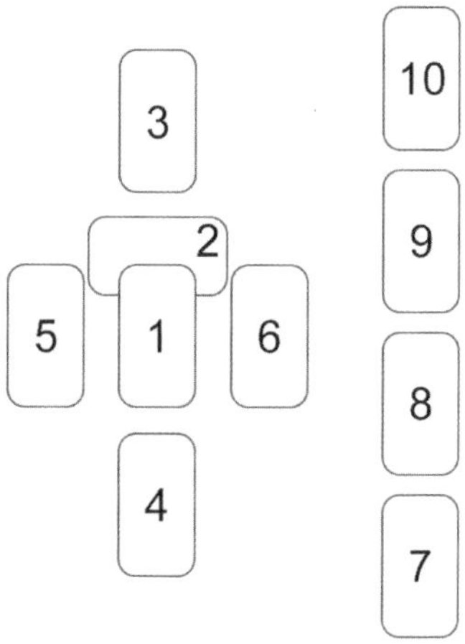

1. The Present or General Sky
2.The Challenge - What's crossing you
3.The Distant Past
4. Recent Past (What's beneath you)
5. What's beside you, or a possible good outcome
6.Immediate Future
7. Inner Feelings
8. External Influences
9.Hopes and Fears
10. Final Outcome.

The Triple Goddess Draw:

(Created especially for The Healing Goddess Oracle Deck)

Get into a meditative or quiet state. Softly ask your question.

Lay out 3 cards in a triangular shape. Place the maiden card on top of the pyramid, the mother and crone cards at the base.

The first card is the **Maiden**- new beginnings, what is fresh and blooming in your life? What brings you excitement and hope?

The second card represents the **Mother**. What is established, significant and currently supporting you? This card is your strength and base of resources. The mother represents what you are already competent in, gifts you bring to the planet.

The last card in the trine is the Crone. This card symbolizes what is transforming in your life. The crone helps you let go of what no longer serves you. Something in life is taking too much energy to sustain. The Crone sometimes brings up fear of loss, but once we allow grief to wash over us, what often follows is relief and release.

Trust is a wonderful quality to embody, while approaching the crone. Behind the curtain of unknown lies new possibility, not yet understood. In the goddess tradition, there is no death, only transformation. In a way, the crone's gift is the largest of all, a peak at our destiny.

The Magic Meditation Technique:

Created especially for The Healing Goddess Oracle Deck.

Attune deeply. Ask your question. Place four cards in a rectangular shape.

Card One- **Commitment**.

Which archetype will help me stay focused and committed on my path. How deep is my commitment? How do I harness the positive side of my commitment?

Card Two- **Intention and Allies.**

What quality or god/goddess energy will help me move forward? How do I use this energy to become empowered? How do I enhance and 'feed' this archetype?

Card Three- **Subconscious Factors.**

What is hidden from me in my subconscious that I need to know to get unstuck? What is it that I need to see in my life to gain better understanding? Does this energy have a shadow side that will undo me? Look to the reversed write up for best subconscious clues. How does knowing this help me?

Card Four-**Outcome**

What outcome may I attract if I keep my commitment, intention and allies nourished? How do I best support myself on this journey?

When using the deck

Take a few moments, breathe deeply, attune to the celestial forces, focus on your question and choose your cards. Feel the meaning that comes through you. Do not feel constrained by the description, if it does not feel applicable. Ask the cards questions. Attune to your intuition to interpret the answers.

Bring your readings to life...

The Goddess and God energies are much like dream figures. To deepen your connection to them, view them as live beings. When any of the guides show up in your reading, visualize them 3 dimensionally. Watch them breathe, walk, blink their eyes. How do they smell? How do they hold space in the room? How do you feel around them? How do they react to you? Speak to them and listen for a reply. The interaction is more meaningful if you see their aliveness. You may call any of them, at any time for further interaction and relationship deepening.

Notice the being's mythical relationship to each other in the layout. This process will be aided if you have knowledge of classical mythology. For example, Zeus and Hera are a royal married couple. Their interactions spark both passion and conflict. Athena is Zeus' favorite daughter. When Zeus aligns with her much is accomplished. Demeter is Persephone's mother and creativity is enhanced when they appear together. Hermes is a messenger. He may bring news to other guides in the deck. So notice if key figures show up together in a reading and reveal their innate relationships. Hold the cards and be their voice. Let them speak to each other. Yes, this much playtime is allowed for adults! It is a great way to hone your intuitive skills.

You may also enrich your experience by inviting the Gods and Goddesses into your dreamtime. Watch for synchronicities, people and events that carry the 'energy' or lessons of the god or goddesses you draw, may show up as humans in waking life. When this happens, pay particular attention to what evolves. When you find the images crossing over into other parts of your life, it affirms your 'knowing' and amplifies the experience.

This deck is meant to enhance your insight, always attune to your own common sense and intuition when reading.

Relax and enjoy... the journey.

References

Aizenstat, Stephen. Dream Lecture, Pacifica University,

Pinkola Estes, Clarissa. The Creative Fire, Myths and Stories on the Cycles of Creativity Audio, Sounds True, 2010

Merlin - Adapted from original artwork by LilKar.

Contents

Gaia - An original illustration by jocokkkk.

0. The Jester—Baubo

Upright:

When Baubo shows up in your cards get ready to laugh! This little being brings the absurd, unexpected and ridiculous! She gives the ability to look at situations differently.

If you are feeling stuck, depressed, or just weary, Baubo is the anti-dote. Spend a little time appreciating the silly, funny and slightly obscene. Get out of your rut and clear your head. Let Baubo lead the way. The Jester energy breaks up stagnation with lightness and laughter, adding her unique touch of unconventional brilliance to each moment.

What could you do right now, to bring some lightness into your day?

Baubo also reminds us that parts of us we are self-conscious about may in time, become our biggest treasures.

A 3rd Century Baubo terracotta figurine from the ancient Greek city of Priene. Card design by Don Saunders.

Reversed:

Are you experiencing an artistic block?

It is time to meet Baubo! She is talented at shaking away stagnation and depression. If you are not having much fun lately, do something to make yourself grin. Do it now! Do not underestimate the power of goofy.

It is so easy to become grim and take one's self very seriously. Laughing at yourself occasionally makes a good healing practice. Baubo in the cards is telling you it is time to shake it up with humor.

Baubo loves spontaneity.

It is playtime!

An original drawing by agsandrew.

1. The Magician—Hermes

Upright:

Time spent with Hermes is always entertaining. When he shows up in your cards something interesting is about to happen. Hermes loves excitement, action and change. He is versatile and teaches you how to adjust to various situations and places. Hermes encourages you to put time into travelling, marketing and sales. He is charming and eloquent and brings talents in writing and speaking.

How can you apply his versatility, ability to communicate and people skills into your personal and business life? Hermes is an alchemist and knows what ingredients to use when creating potions, group dynamics and ideas. It's not just about what you have, but how you blend it! How can you artfully combine what is already yours, to create something fresh and relevant? Hermes also brings newness and change. What fresh ideas are bursting through you?

From *Mercury* painted by Hendrick Goltius in 1611.
Card design by: Don Saunders.

Reversed:

Hermes can be both bluntly honest and purposely deceptive. Has he left you confused? Look to actions, not words to see the truth. Do not be fooled by charm; it is a magician's trick. Hermes ego is fragile and he gets a little mean when confronted or snubbed. He may also meddle, gossip and create mischief. The best way back from Herme's fun, but short ride is through your heart. Get in touch with what matters, not with what sounds best. Own your part in the deception. Was there a small part of you that enjoyed travelling with the magic man? Keep your inner magician alive by learning from his ingenuity and flexibility. Apply these skills to your personal magic bag.

Hermes and Pegasus from *Parnassus*
painted by Andrea Mantegna in 1497

2. The High Priestess—Persephone

Upright:

When Persephone enters your cards, you know you are in the realm of inspiration. Persephone is imaginative and mystical. She manifests potions, visions, hopes and new dimensions. Like her mentor Hekate, Persephone is able to cross thresholds. She is comfortable in both the inky recesses of the underworld and the stark brightness of the upperworld. When Persephone is in your life, you are able to see in the dark. Nothing enduring is made without incorporating two strands, one of shadows and one of illumination. True originality requires both ends of the spectrum to unfold. Persephone also brings deep insights. She understands how your thoughts and feelings pave your life path. She comes to you in dream state and visions to pass her knowledge on. Attune to her nightly updates to see the unique knowledge the High Priestess gives to you. What did you dream last night? Do any of the feelings match what is happening in your life? How so? Why is that important?

From an original drawing by Ellerslie.
Card design by Don Saunders.

Reversed:

If you are in a creative slump feed your inner high priestess. She is nourished by myths, colors, beautiful surroundings and being attentive to your dreams. Do not discount the synchronicities and magic that show up in your daily life. This is how she manifests. Sometimes Persephone's insights follow a depression. What you learn from these dark, inner voyages can be life-changing revelations. Learn to harvest the insight from your descent. Dealing with Persephone takes tolerance for ambiguity. Write down what you remember and learn before it fades. Part of Persephone's shadow reveals a self -destructive streak. When on a journey with Persephone, balance the needs of your inner mystic with staying grounded. On Persephone's watch, it can be hard to maintain daily life. Yet, the high priestess needs you to keep both your body and spiritual life nourished. Are you initiating new visions in your life? How so? Are you maintaining day-to-day realities? If not, does anything need to change?

Proserpine or Persephone
painted by Dante Gabriel Rossetti in 1874

3. The Empress—Hera

Upright:

When the Queen of Heavens graces you with her presence she is granting you the gift of partnership and devotion. She is a phenomenal spouse and values deep, respectful relationships. Hera is monogamous and keeps her promises, even when it is inconvenient. She is able to be strong and supportive at the same time. She is reminding you to count your blessings and be grateful for the intimate partnership you have. No spouse is perfect, but remember why you fell in love with yours. What special gifts do they bring? If you are single, Hera may bring a potential mate your way, or may be nudging you to appreciate your own company more. Enjoy the sensuality and luxury of your life. Hera respects those who live up to their promises. Make your word gold.

3. The Empress

Hera

From an original painting by Paula Pesonen.
Card design by Don Saunders

Reversed:

Hera is a devoted wife, but betrayals have left her angry, vengeful and bitter.

Is there anywhere in your life you are feeling betrayed? Are you seething and unable to let to of your resentment? If so, confront the one who cheated on you. If you wish to stay with them, you will need to forgive. If you cannot forgive, do not stay. If you are choosing a mate, look for someone whose loyalty, devotion and commitment equal your own. Do not squash your own significant power for the idea of a relationship. Be sure the person is deserving of the many gifts you offer. Honor time you spend with yourself. You are a person of means and integrity. Keep your commitment for another in reserve, until you know they are worthy. Relax and forgive the past. The present is made better when you flow with what is and show gratitude.

Hera (with crown) in
The Judgment of Paris
painted by Anton Raphael Mends
around 1757

4. The Emperor—Zeus

Upright:

When Zeus shows up in your cards, you are holding a royal hand.

The King of Gods is surging with currents of power and experience. Zeus brings optimism, lust for life and lots of energy. He lets you know you can accomplish anything!

What is your desire?

He creates new ideas and projects through his positive interactions. Zeus brings abundance, good fortune and manifestation. If you want to establish a business or endeavor, this is the time. Zeus is a dynamic administrator. If you wish to increase your competence and status, his charisma is an undeniable asset.

Zeus is a strong and magnetic force. Tap into your own allure and draw in, what is of great benefit for all aspects of your life.

From an original drawing by Elena Terletskaya.
Card design by: Don Saunders.

Reversed:

Are you acting like a dictator in any way? If you want to hear the truth from others, then, do not punish them when they tell it to you. Zeus brings plenty of charm and potential. Whatever he touches is changed by his power. The lightening he generates can be fodder for destruction or brilliant manifestation. Practice being mindful about what you focus on.

With great power, comes great responsibility. How will your actions affect the lives of others? Use your influence wisely. Ensure your thoughts and actions create a positive outcome for all.

Jupiter
in a wall painting from Pompeii

5. The Healer—Asclepius

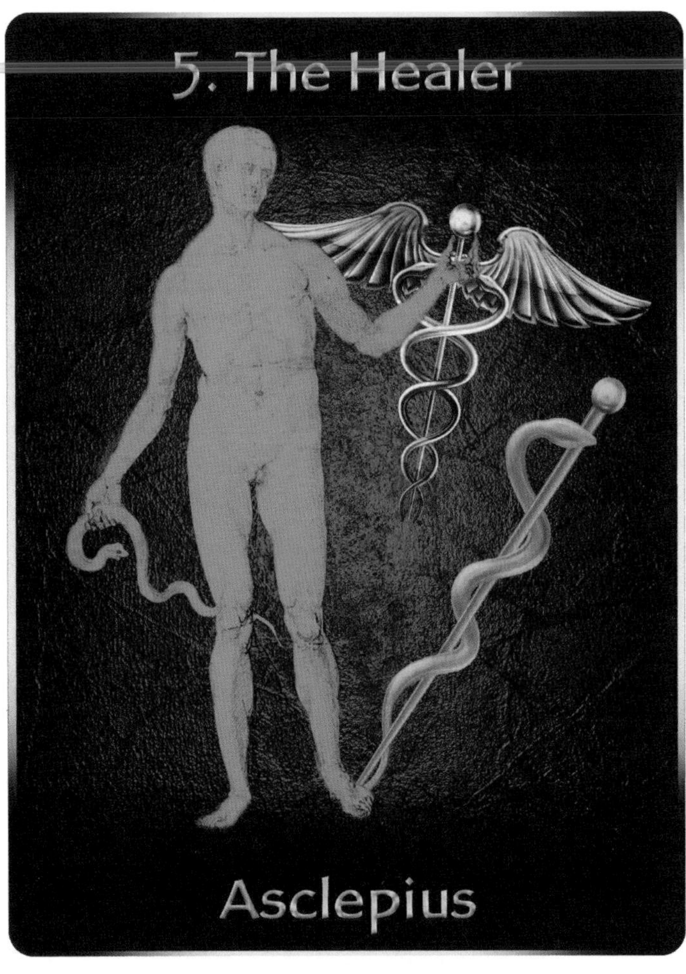

From *Asclepius* painted by
Albrecht Dürer (1471-1528).
Card design by Don Saunders.

Upright:

When Asclepius shows up in your reading you are being given the opportunity to heal. Your body is skilled at maintaining stasis and repairing itself. If you attune, or meditate, it will tell you what to do. Celebrate in your body's brilliance. Asclepius also heals others. You may be asked to give your time and attention to help another while they are vulnerable. This son of Apollo accomplished great medical feats. His staff, a snake symbolizes deep regeneration and medical excellence. Asclepius in your cards brings you, your own miracle. Align with your higher good and wish for something powerful!

Reversed:

You may be asked to take time and decipher the message your body is giving you. What does it need? What do you require on an emotional, mental and spiritual level? How do you align your body and mind so they can work together more harmoniously?

Asclepius reversed may be reminding you to attend to the balance in your life. Are you ignoring or misusing your innate power to heal? Are you doing what you really want in life? Are you doing what you are meant to do?

Setbacks are a way of pressing the reset button in the psyche providing another chance to align with what you want at your core. You are being given precious knowledge, at one time considered forbidden. Ensure you use it for the highest good.

If you are caretaking another, who is sick, it may feel like a burden, but you have the power to make that time into a healing and transforming experience, for all parties involved.

A statue of *Asclepius*
found among the ruins of Ampurias, Spain

6. The Lovers—Aphrodite

Upright:

When Aphrodite enters your life, take the time to relax and become aligned. Her message is to play more and worry less. She brings gifts of beauty and pleasure, which give life texture and meaning. Breathe in her appreciation for magnificence and allow her to transform drudgery to ease. Open your senses and smell, taste, touch, hear and see all the abundance around you. Aphrodite blesses you with love, happiness and laughter. Her presence helps you awaken to what is precious. Aphrodite teaches you to be thankful for your many gifts. She knows how to romance the moment and sparks your enthusiasm for life. If you are single, the Lovers card indicates romance is just a dream away. If you are married, she reminds you to take the time to listen to and appreciate your mate.

From an original drawing by Liliya Kulianionak.
Card design by Don Saunders.

Reversed:

Are you making good choices in your love life? Do the people in your life let you be yourself? Do you feel appreciated for who you are? Do you do enough of what gives you bliss and joy? If not, how can you?

On the other hand, are you over indulging and ignoring your responsibilities? Are you respecting the needs of others? Are you being truthful in difficult situations?

Aphrodite teaches you that your life is a series of potentially amazing moments. You will never have this exact experience again. You are the powerful creator of your life. It is important to balance work, play, truth and kindness.

Be cognizant of how your choices create your life. The creative palette Aphrodite offers is comprised of beauty, sensuality, enjoyment, romance and gratitude. Do not rush through her lessons of love relaxation and pleasure. They are precious and sweet.

The Birth of Venus
painted by William-Adolphe Bouguereau in 1897.

7. The Chariot—Achilles

From *The Triumph of Achilles in Corfu*
painted by Franz Matsch in 1892
Card design by Don Saunders.

Upright:

When you receive Achilles in an upright position you are being gifted with energy, focus and willpower. Achilles brings hope, heroic effort and momentum.

You have strength, purpose and strategic ability. You are able to work hard and accomplish much. You may be asked to help with social causes. It is a good time to step up and defend others. It is the time to move your projects, ideas and life forward. The Chariot gives you much ability to manifest. This will be true with your physical, emotional and spiritual energy, as long as it is aligned with your highest purpose. You are brave and loyal, but not invulnerable. Balance is still vital. Pay attention to the needs of your body and messages from those around you. Tap into your wisdom to know when to engage and when to regenerate. How do you wish to use your drive to move your life forward, now?

Reversed:

A reversed Achilles suggests it is time to realistically assess where you are vulnerable. Which part of your body and emotions is sending you messages to slow down and pay attention? What is your body telling you? How can you help to heal yourself? This is the time to tend to a wounded part of your life. Caring for yourself now will allow you to resume later, with even more wisdom and purpose. The Achilles card advises you to use your power wisely. Think things through and act with purpose and heart, not vengeance or anger. If you are blinded by love or rage, it could have negative effects. Be careful to not allow negative impulses to override your wiser knowing. You have plenty of drive and momentum, but focus your wisdom before moving in any direction to avoid setbacks.

The Wrath of Achilles painted by François-Léon Benouville in 1847

8. Strength—Psyche

Upright:

The type of strength held by Psyche is not always exalted. Yet, without the hard earned talents of discretion, persistence and patience we are unable to make our lives shine in an enduring way. None of these skills is easily developed. They require practicing tasks and attitudes that are difficult to cultivate. Yet, when Psyche shows up in your cards she is asking you, "how badly do you want, what you say you want"? For Psyche, the prize was winning back the love of her husband Eros.

From *Psyche in the Underworld*
painted by Paul Alfred de Curzon (1820-1895)
Card design by Don Saunders.

The ordeal she needed to accomplish turned her into a woman of substance and skill. So when you are faced with tasks that seem boring or difficult, ask, "how are they developing the deeper aspects of my character?" Stick to worthy pursuits to become a person of integrity. True love of course, is always your finest strength. The picture reveals Psyche bringing a box back from the underworld. What would you risk everything to have? Why is this so important to you?

Cupid and Psyche painted by Adolphe-William Bouguereau in 1889

Reversed:

Part of discretion is determining if what you are doing will serve a greater purpose, or teach you worthy skills. Are you making good choices in your life? Are your choices leading you to where you wish to be? Do you keep your eye on your goal, or get off track and forget your purpose? Psyche reminds you to keep a clear head about what you are doing and why you are doing it. Are you persistent enough, or do you give up easily? If your goals and schedule accomplish what is of value to you, they are worthy.

What gives you strength and purpose? Feed this part of yourself. Do not forget to celebrate your successes. Accomplishment will feel satisfying, if it meets needs that are real and meaningful. Success will feel hollow if the original goal was someone else's, or not of true importance to you. It takes patience and persistence to face your fear and accomplish goals. This takes strength- so does love.

9. The Hermit—Hephaestus

9. The Hermit

Hephaestus

From *Der Parnaß*
painted by Andrea Mantegna in 1497
Card design by Don Saunders.

Upright:

Hephaestus teaches you to accept yourself, warts, wounds and beauty. This is not a task that comes easily for most of us. You can knock yourself out trying to please someone who does not really 'get' you, but it won't help, if you are not who they love. Someone will always find reasons to reject or find fault. Yet, it is by daring to be yourself, that your own unique brilliance is honed. Sometimes you need to be alone for extensive periods to get to know and appreciate yourself. You need time and training to develop skills that allow you to bring your gifts into the light and claim your own power. Hephaestus grants you time alone. He also brings artistic skills and intelligence. What are the gifts you are forging from your disappointments and upsets? How are you turning them into amazing assets?

Reversed:

It hurts when someone you love does not love you back, or see your strengths. It is crippling to be rejected and ignored. Yet, in order to develop a sense of self, you need to love even your wounds and less than perfect pieces. Seeing and accepting, your damaged parts develops character and depth. It makes you whole and unstoppable. If you do not take the time to turn self-hate into love, you will be perpetually bitter and angry. Learning to forgive those who have hurt you with their rejection and indifference, grants you freedom. How have your feelings of unworthiness been harming you? Where did these wounds start? You have the power to stop the self-punishing. How can you accept yourself fully and embrace your worthiness? Take time alone to restore perspective and sanity.

Vulcan forging the rays of Jupiter
painted by Peter Paul Rubens in 1636

10. The Wheel of Life—Eros

Upright:

When Eros comes knocking it is time to put on your finest attire and open the door. Eros brings passion. The zeal may be for a person, an idea or a lifestyle. Even though, a visit by Eros is often unexpected, it will ignite something new and lead you in a fun and provocative direction. The arrows of Eros are special. They change perspective and open up new fortune. By following your heart, new pieces of yourself blossom, as do new opportunities. Eros also teaches wisdom about surviving the ride on the wheel of life. Every position has up and down points. Learn to love where you are. Being in the present moment allows enjoyment and acceptance. Fighting the ride is natural initially, but continuous resistance creates an anxious journey. What is bringing you passion? Who is offering love?

From *Cupid and Psyche* painted in 1891
by Annie Louisa Robinson Swynnerton
Card design by Don Saunders

Cupidon painted in 1891
by William-Adolphe Bouguereau

Reversed:

It is important to pursue love, with clarity, not naivety. Sometimes, it is a short ride that does not last. If you have had a bad experience, know that the wound created by Eros's arrow, will hold the medicine. There will be much to learn and understand from meditating on the experience. Regardless of where Eros takes you, you need to come back to yourself, and direct real love and empathy in your own direction. Eros teaches the only place to be on the wheel of fortune is 'where you are currently at'. Wishing to be somewhere else, with someone else creates anxiety and dissatisfaction. Make your life choices wisely then realize every ride has high points and bumps. If you are in a committed relationship avoid being fickle. Even if your indiscretion is not exposed, you cheapen your relationship with thoughtless actions. However, a little objectivity and humor is a valuable asset on the ever-changing wheel of life.

11. Justice—Athena

From an original drawing by Kuco
Card design by Don Saunders.

Upright:

When Athena shows up in your life know you are in the hands of a great mentor. The Goddess of Justice wants you to define your goals. She is an academic and encourages you to get the education you need to excel. Get clear on what your talents and interests are and determine how to use them in the workforce. She is also fiercely independent economically and may suggest you find a business or career that is relatively lucrative. She is inventive and practical. No matter what your situation, she knows you can shine and encourages you to work both hard and smart. She will help steer you in the direction of making strategic business decisions. She brings great ability to be resourceful and clever. Athena is a visionary. Like the bird in the drawing she sees into the future. What plans do you have to implement your ideas and skills? Athena also solidifies your relationship to older males, such as your father. She is loyal a good negotiator and has strong decision making ability. Athena is very fair and brings justice into her personal and professional life. How are you able to create equitable relationships in your situation?

Reversed:

It may be time to get out of your head and pay attention to your heart. Have you been armored in your relationships, lately? Is there an issue of trust going on? If so, get clear on what you want. Athena reversed insists you think strategically about your business and career. A good plan and consistent implementation aids success. Performance is rewarded when the student learns how to master a subject. This takes patience, practice and humility. Showing proper respect and loyalty toward your mentors creates good relationships and future dealings. If you are financially, self-sufficient consider helping those in need of economic and skill based resources. Athena may bring material reward, and recognition, but she insists you work ethically. Athena is not a cuddly goddess. She brings fairness and justice. If you have been cutting corners, it is time to stop and make amends.

Athena Scorning the Advances of Hephaestus painted around 1560 by Paris Bordone

12. The Paradox—Pan

Upright:

When Pan shows up in your cards it is time to take a walk on the wild side. Sometimes perspectives need to change. Pan knows how to take you out of your comfort zone and introduce a little feral blood into your veins. The old goat is charismatic and unconventional. He is drawn to inner paradoxes. Where are you saying one thing and doing another? Becoming uptight when too much is expected of you and bowing to social convention can cause damage. Sometimes you just have to say what you really want, rather than pretending. Evading a confrontation will cause ripples of reaction to become waves of anger, if not dealt with. Pan does believe in right and wrong, but in an organic approach, not predicated by conventional norms. So if you are feeling too constrained, this wild card may help you find freedom through the unusual. Pan is also giving you an invitation to explore the world of nature. It can wake you up and give you perspective.

From an original drawing by Kenzie Volkov
Card design by Don Saunders.

A 1914 illustration of *Pan* from *The Story of Greece* by Mary McGregor

Reversed:

Have you been in a rut and unwilling to try something new? Pan suggests it is time to start seeing what is fresh and magical. That does not mean the routine you have been following is not worthy, but maybe you have stopped being appreciative. Falling asleep in your life is akin to death. So, wake up and evaluate what needs to shift. As a wise man once said, "you can change two things in your life, your situation or your attitude". Both choices are indeed powerful. What needs to be made congruent in your life? Where are you not walking your talk?

Get congruent. If you have been living a lie, it is time to admit the truth and take the consequences. Pan is not a fan of hypocrisy. A trip to his temple, nature, will help you clear the cobwebs and prioritize what is important.

13. The Crossroads—Hekate

13. The Crossroads

Hekate

From an original drawing
by Jo Ann Hammond Meiers
Card design by Don Saunders.

Upright:

When the triple goddess, Hekate shows up in your cards it is time to close a chapter of your life. Ask yourself truthfully, 'what no longer serves me'? Nature knows how to prune off what is no longer vital. When an apple tree has too many small apples to effectively support, it sheds some. If it did not, the tree itself, and all of its other baby apples would die. We feel dead or stuck when we refuse to make choices that are uncomfortable. Is there a choice you need to make that you are avoiding? There is no perfect path. All choices at the crossroads carry risks and have a price. Indecision is a type of purgatory and staleness is the price. Hekate can give you the tools to see your options. Choose with your heart and instinct intact and move forward. Cerberus the 3-headed dog recognizes the smell of truth. Have him sniff your decision before implementation to detect any deception. After the deed is done, or over, letting go of what you tried so hard to hang on to can actually feel like a relief.

Reversed:

Hekate gives you the opportunity to be truthful about what and whom you need in your life, to meet your soul purpose. You cannot move on to a new chapter, until you close an old one. When you do not willingly make decisions, sometimes fate will do it for you. Old situations and relationships may dissolve or explode or Illness or disaster may occur. What is it you need to let go of? Why are you really hanging on? There is a non-negotiable quality about Hekate. Nevertheless, she is also a teacher of great power.

When you no longer belong in one realm, she can show you how to navigate the next. All things change and many cannot be controlled. She teaches you to allow in a new cycle, and see the gifts that it brings. No matter where you journey, Hekate makes an unparalleled mentor, who guides the way.

Hecate: Procession to a Witches' Sabbath
painted by Jusepe de Ribera (1591–1652)

14. The Inner Sanctuary—Hestia

Upright:

Hestia, goddess of the hearth is showing up to boost your self-worth. This guide brings the ability to find what you need inside of yourself. She teaches you to tend your inner sanctuary. What is it that truly excites you? What makes the light shine brighter in your eyes? This passion is the one to feed and nourish. Do not get side tracked by lesser desires that only consume you. She teaches balance, good judgment and how to keep the inner temple sacred. Hestia likes to go slow. She is strong enough to know her deliberate rhythm, is important and nurturing. Hestia sees the good in others, even when society forgets them. Her belief in people helps free them from addictions, and self sabotage. Hestia carries true kindness and hospitability. Hestia quietly respects her own self worth, and the worth of others.

Reversed:

Hestia shows you that you are the creator of your own life, from the tiniest thought to the largest action. You hold incredible power! The keys are to keep your inner fire burning and tend to your inner cycles.

From *The Flame Goddess of Fire* painted by Odilon Redon in 1896 Card design by Don Saunders.

An original drawing by Tatiana Toutheou

Learning to see where you are in the season of your soul leads you toward deeper understanding, of your own growth process. There are times when you are in winter mode. You are hibernating and regenerating. Trying to disrupt your slumber pattern at this time would only stunt your growth. Hestia teaches you patience. Certain things cannot be rushed. Hestia also carries the Olympian Flame to remind you of your significance. At times, you feel invisible, as if your talents and contributions are not seen or appreciated. Learn to take this matter into your own hands. Witness your own accomplishments and feel your worth, fully, quietly and internally. This is a super power few people attain. You are no longer at the mercy of others to validate you.

15. The Underworld — Hades

From an original drawing by Fotokostic
Card design by Don Saunders.

Upright:

When Hades appears in a reading pay close attention to your senses. Is there something that you are not noticing that you need to focus on? Is anything too good to be true? Hades can be a part of ourselves that self sabotages. Hades can also be an outer force that negates or harms your creative life and soul purpose.

There are three major reasons we do not confront Hades:

1. We do not see his mischief, as our senses are not developed to detect what is awry.

2. We comply with the self-destructive energy, because it in some way makes our life easier, or pleases our ego.

3. We are scared and do not know what to do to stop this force.

Where is Hades appearing in your life? How can you find, track and stop him. When Hades enters your cards, it is time to wake up, determine what is challenging your growth and put an end to his power.

Reversed:

Hades has tricked us and taken away something we love. The Hades force is often a piece of us that does not believe we are worthy. This inner force will then cause us to behave, as if its negative voice is true. For example, even if we are prepared for an important meeting we get sick before it happens, and lose an opportunity. Hades may also manifest as an outer adversary, such as, a deal, we strike with our boss, at work. We agree to work more time for more money. We become successful financially, but our personal life becomes flat and feels less meaningful. When Hades arrives, it is important to figure out his sabotage, where he hides and how to stop him. You are wise enough to see his tricks. Pay attention and stop the destruction!

Hades from an original drawing by Koco

16. The Tower — Medusa

Upright:

From an original drawing by YorkBerlin
Card design by Don Saunders.

When Medusa shows up in your cards keep alert. It is very easy to be blamed and rejected when others do not understand you, or your situation. You may have been held responsible for someone else's mistake or convicted for acts you did not carry out. Try not to get defensive and escalate the discord. However, do not fall victim to unfair accusations. Remember, Medusa is a target because she has great capacity. What is your power? When you learn to use self-reflection as a tool, to witness and accept all parts of yourself, you become very strong. As one of the fierce gorgon sisters Medusa carries immortal blood. She can bring the dead back to life. How can you use this life giving energy to find a piece of yourself, you thought was lost? What can you do today to accept yourself, wholly and completely? How can you use patience and clarity and be more understood? How can you use your regenerative, snake-power to see deeply into your life?

Reversed:

Medusa brings the unexpected! Yes, sometimes things fall apart in our lives and it creates chaos, confusion and upset. Yet, without our foundations occasionally breaking, we would not have a reason to evolve. We need to trust that we are strong enough to get to the other side of this occurrence.

Sometimes we are victim to other's prejudice and meanness. Nevertheless, the person who lives through such bias and turns it into understanding, becomes powerful indeed! It does not hurt to take a glimpse at why you have such a strong impact on others. Gain some insight about group dynamics, but do not give up your unique identity. Looking into a mirror can be uncomfortable, but insightful.

What do you see when you self-reflect? Turn your objective insights into growth.

Medusa painted by Carlos Schwabe in 1895

17. The Star—Metis

Upright:

Metis is the original wisdom goddess. She was Zeus' first spouse. He said he cared about her, but tricked her into making herself small and swallowed her. He chose power over his relationship with her, and she paid the price. When Metis shows up in your cards she is reminding you, how wise and intelligent you are. She is showing you, your potential to use strategy and intuition in your life. You can reach for the stars and follow your aspirations, when they are true. This is the time to play it big and put your genius out there. What are your talents? Where in your life can you use your skills? Do not give up on your own dreams for the sake of anyone else. Sometimes our bright starlight is what others use to see their way. They do not always see where this light originates. Your wisdom is very special. See this gift in yourself and make good decisions.

From an original painting by Paula Pesonen
Card design by Don Saunders.

Reversed:

If the hair on the back of your neck is tingling and you know a situation is not right, pay attention to your instincts. What is not feeling right to you, at this time? Do not get tricked into making yourself small and invisible to please someone else or avoid conflict. Instead, pay heed to your own wisdom, right now! Many crimes are committed when unscrupulous people take advantage of other's kindness and politeness. Do not put manners ahead of good sense.

Others who try to make you less visible or important are not really your friends. They are putting their own egos ahead of their relationship with you. Do not be trapped in that game and be harmed by their tricks. In addition, it is good to acknowledge the genius in other's without jealousy, or comparison. We are all unique stars. Your ability to shine brightly allows other stars to become visible. It in no way diminishes their shine.

A scene from a black figured amphora dating between 550 and 525 BC.
After he swallowed her pregnant mother, Metis, Athena is "born" from Zeus' forehead.

18. The Moon—Artemis

Upright:

When the moon goddess shows up in your cards she nudges you toward freedom. Artemis values her space. She likes to spend time doing what she loves. She wants you to remember who you really are and what resonates with you at your deepest level. She brings you glimpses of your soul essence. Artemis reminds you of your unique talents and purpose. Honor her arrival by scheduling time to revisit your needs. She also encourages visiting your mother's people. What gifts did you inherit from your mother's family? Artemis loves to walk outdoors, take in fresh air and be independent. How might you make wild, free time for yourself, today? The Moon also reminds you of your natural cycles. Much benefit results when you claim the right to live in your natural rhythm. What projects, people and ideas are ripe for exploration?

From an original painting by Paula Pesonen
Card design by Don Saunders.

Reversed:

When Artemis shows up reversed she wants to know if you are feeling caged in? Signs of feeling restricted may include resentment and irritability. If these are present ask, "what do I really need to do, say and admit today, to be my true self?" Artemis may also push away what matters, such as love, by being too competitive. Her tendency to tell the truth may also become fierce. Give clear messages, but deliver them with kindness, including your self-talk. Also, be sure you are attuning to your rhythms and working with your internal cycles. Being free to be authentic and feel self-respect, without any oppression is what Artemis most values.

Artemis standing beside Endymon from a 1915 illustration by Helen Stratton for *A Book of Myths*

19. The Sun — Apollo

19. The Sun

Apollo

From an original drawing
by Jo Ann Hammond-Meiers
and *Apollo Vanquishing the Serpent Python*
painted by Gustave Moreau in 1885
Card design by Don Saunders.

Upright:

When Apollo enters your life, he brings sunshine. Apollo wields perspective and illumination. If you have been fuzzy headed you will now have clarity.

Apollo sees all and knows what is going on. If you have a need to get to the root of what has been holding you back, Apollo can offer answers. His high perspective allows him to know how any issue in your life started and evolved. He values truth and clean action.

What would you like to see more clearly in your life? Apollo brings energy into your day. He can help you look at challenges in a logical and realistic way. This can lead to moving forward in areas where you felt stuck.

Apollo is also courageous in his beliefs and takes on authority figures if they are deceitful or self-serving. His presence brings healing.

Reversed:

You may need to wait a bit longer to see the full story on an issue that has been blocking you, but you are close.

Remember to ask relevant questions. What do I wish to see clearly? Who can best help me? Who has perspective and knowledge? Apollo can be blunt when he delivers truth. He can also be a harsh judge. If his communication comes as criticism, keep perspective. Find the jewel in the message and let the rest dissipate, without harming you. Sometimes the truth does set us free, even though it initially feels shattering.

Apollo and the Muses
painted by Simon Vouet in 1640

20. Wise Response—Poseidon

Upright:

When Poseidon shows up in your life, use your sense of discretion. This means discern right from wrong and make up your own mind. Do not be bluffed by statistics or big emotions. Balance facts with deeper knowing. Take time to figure things out, before you react. Instead, respond wisely, to create a better outcome. What are you reacting to, that you would be better off responding to thoughtfully?

You have intuition surfacing at this time. Bring it to the surface through your dreams. Attend to your deep feelings and notice synchronicities Let these charmed universal messages show you when you are on the right path. Poseidon also brings psychic connections. Look for magic in the everyday.

From *Neptune and Amphitrite*
painted by Paris Bordone in 1560
Card design by Don Saunders.

Reversed:

The judgment we carry deep inside of us creates much of our own destiny. If we unconsciously feel angry with ourselves, we will self-punish or self-sabotage. Things will not work out and we will blame fate. When we are pleased with ourselves, we unconsciously clear our own path. What are your subconscious feelings creating in your life? Poseidon's moisture is magnificent for watering what is dry in your life. However, unbridled emotion can cause extensive damage. A few minutes of dysfunction can undo year's worth of good will. Breathe and think of the consequences. Remember which relationships you value and do not destroy them, because of an angry outburst.

Then decide how to respond, getting your point across, without obliterating others. Poseidon brings great mystery, but can create confusion. Patience helps to untangle, what is real from what is illusion. Do not be hasty in your reactions.

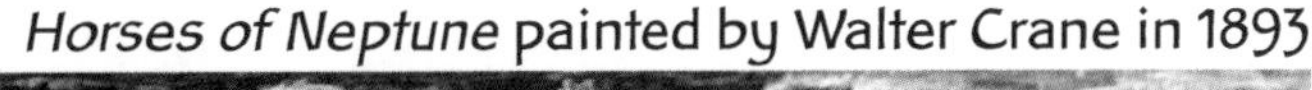

Horses of Neptune painted by Walter Crane in 1893

21 The Great Mother—Demeter

21. The Great Mother

Demeter

From an original drawing by Katalinks
Card design by Don Saunders.

Upright:

When Demeter shows up in your cards the great mother is embracing you. She gives you nurturing, reassurance and love. Demeter holds secrets of birth, death and every cycle in between. Her presence helps to restore rhythm. She helps you learn the laws of nature. There is man made law, which is conducted at the courts. Then there is Demeter's law, or karma. Start focusing on natural law within your own body and life. Attend to eating well, sleeping well and being calm. Demeter's arrival may also bless you with abundance and fertility.

Watch your dreams for the arrival of babies, plants and birth. If the dream babies or plants are healthy, so is your new development. If the images show up as sick or dead, ask, "what in me now is unable to hold new life,"? How can I remedy that situation? Demeter also shows you it is natural to go from up to down, young to old. Exposure to her varied experiences helps you become whole and rich. Demeter is heart based and each of her visits brings generosity and tenderness.

Reversed:

When the great mother is reversed, she wants you to pay attention to your body. Are you working late? It is time to slow down, get some sleep and attend to your nutrition. Eat fresh, green foods, drink green smoothies and breathe in fresh air. Demeter is not a fan of a mechanized, fast paced world. Let go of the multi-tasking, list making and corporate agenda. She finds it's dehumanizing and skews your priorities. Do not waste your life chasing status. Move into your heart and find out what you really want. Nurture children around you, or your inner child. Spend time around plants, small animals and babies of any sort. Pay attention to your grief. What is crying out inside of you? What has real meaning to you? How will you know when it feels right?

Demeter mourning Persephone
painting by Evelyn De Morgan in 1906.

22. Shaman of Earth—Changing Woman

Upright:

When Changing Woman comes into your cards, it indicates you are yearning for growth. You are choosing a new path that will allow you to develop and use more of your skills.

Turn to her for instruction. Think clearly, about what you want. What do you want to change?

She is a teacher of plant medicine and Shamanic journeying techniques. Learn skills, such as these to grow your intuition stronger and to tap into her wisdom.

Study the weather, the clouds, plants and animals around you for deeper understanding of her clues.

You will find your competence and confidence increase, as you are able to decipher the messages nature provides.

From an original painting by Greg Clark, Arizona.
Card design by Don Saunders.

Reversed:

You are in a state of transformation, but you may be hesitating. Changing Woman assures you that 'resistance is futile'. You do not always get the choice. Participating in nature's shifts makes the process easier.

As humans, we do not control life's phases. Sometimes the best we can do is to adjust to our new circumstances and relax into the process. Like the caterpillar, we must just trust that what is happening will ultimately have a favorable outcome.

From an original painting by Bruce Rolff

23. Maven of Earth—Baba Yaga

From an original photograph by Laurin Rinder
Card design by Don Saunders.

Upright:

When Baba Yaga shows up in your cards you are being tested. She is interested in assessing your skill level. There may be difficult tasks in front of you.

Baba Yaga is very powerful and mysterious. She wants you to prove your survival skills and inner resourcefulness. Baba Yaga is not interested in you 'talking the talk'. She likes tangible evidence of how you think and act under pressure. If you are able to stay calm, be sensible and not ask more than you need to know, you may survive her stringent training.

It is important to represent yourself as you are, not more, not less. When dealing with Baba Yaga, stay humble, but not invisible. Keep your wits about you and you will graduate. Baba Yaga rewards her students with self-knowledge and worldly wisdom. You will be hard to fool or intimidate after her training.

Reversed:

If you ask a favor of the Maven of Earth you'd better be prepared to meet her demands. If you are applying for a new school, or new job be sure you are ready to put in the time, money and commitment. Do not start programs that will advance you, unless you are ready to work hard and make the changes necessary. This is also true of relationships. Baba Yaga likes to see integrity and clear intention. Think before you leap. Do not make promises you cannot keep. Be prepared and be truthful.

You will succeed if you truly commit yourself.

Baba Yaga
from an illustration for the book *Vasilissa the Beautiful*
drawn by Ivan Yakovlevich Bilibin in 1900

24. Magi of Earth—Gaia

Upright:

Gaia brings possibility and abundance. She is the original mother, who created everyone and everything. Through merging with darkness, The Magi of Earth birthed light. The ultimate creatrix, comes to tell you that, "inside you dwells great possibilities." She urges you to find your original nature. Tap into mythology, dreams and ancient legends. From the rawest part of your being, what do you birth?

From an original drawing by Ellerslie
Card design by Don Saunders.

Gaia can produce with any medium. Mud, imagination and loneliness, are a few of her building materials. Do not restrict your creativity because you think your tools are not good enough. Construct with what you have, now. Gaia is primal potential. She knows anything is possible. She knows no limits. Reawaken your sense of connection to the rivers, wind, earth and fire- all her children. Know each of these elements live inside of you. All inspire, all sustain.

Reversed:

Have you been holding back on your inventiveness? Have you judged and criticized your work until it shrivels? Gaia shows you how to open to possibilities. Shut down the 'shoulds' and 'doubts' that hold you back. Instead, create for the sake of creating.

The Magi of Earth reversed is also a reminder that we do not have to be restricted by, or bow to our manifestations. If someone or something we helped becomes ungrateful or malicious, we can sever the relationship. Do not suffer because you lack the boundary ability to say 'no more'. Where in your life do you need to say, 'no more'?

Gaia from a ceiling painted in 1875 by Anselm Feuerbach in the Academy of Fine Arts, Vienna

25. Shaman of Air—Arthur

Arthur painted by Charles Earnest Butler in 1903
Card design by Don Saunders.

Upright:

The appearance of Arthur suggests a great adventure awaits you. It is time for exploration. What are the pressing questions in your mind? What is important that you need to take care of? It is time for you to seek, travel, and take in what the world has to offer.

Even if you are not young in age, this is a chance to renew your excitement about possibilities. Arthur is also a bridge between old and new ways of thinking. It is important to be thoughtful and keep what is significant when establishing your personal traditions. It is also time to bring in new ideas that will rejuvenate your life.

Arthur searches for love and immortality. What are you searching for? What is your holy grail?

Reversed:

If you feel stagnant, you can make a change. You must get off the couch and out of your house to bring in new energy. Allow yourself to be curious.

Doing the same thing over and over and expecting a different result, 'is insanity', according to Einstein.

Instead, try a new approach and take a beneficial risk. Try a fun activity to improve your health.

What feels hollow and wrong in your life?

Re-examine your priorities. Are they still fresh and relevant? What has great significance?

Fill your holy grail and drink deeply from that which keeps you fulfilled.

Arthur
from an Illustration in *The Boy's King Arthur*,1922

26. Maven of Air—Sophia

Upright:

Sophia brings deep wisdom. Her knowledge is rare. It is the result of integrating feelings and deep understanding of the world. She rewards maturity, empathy and clarity. Sophia is all seeing. She is the part of you that is able to speak to the goddess directly. She is your deep sense of knowing. Sophia illuminates your soul purpose. The Maven of Air is universal. She rises above biases and prejudices. Her love is unshakable and unconditional. Sophia knows you are capable of weaving a thread of compassion into each day. She knows your contribution is important.

Become still and attune to Sophia. Receive instructions on how to use your talents to contribute to the world every day. What is she telling you, right now?

Reversed:

This is the time to look at the big picture of your life. Do a review of what your major events and lessons have been. When did they happen? How did they change you?

From an original drawing by Atelier Sommerland
Card design by Don Saunders.

Integrate lessons from your ancestors. What did they sacrifice for your freedom? You are the vessel for all of their hopes and dreams. How can you move forward and realize these?

Sophia reminds you that information is not knowledge. Knowledge must be earned through practice and competency. This only happens with persistence, focus and dedication. She asks you to commit to what you are here to do. Go through the apprenticeship and learn your trade.

There are no shortcuts to wisdom.

From an original drawing by Majcot

27. Magi of Air—Merlin

From a 1916 illustration of
Merlin The Mysterious Stranger by N. C. Wyeth
Card design by Don Saunders.

Upright:

Merlin is a splendid teacher of science and astronomy. He opens you up to possibilities. This wizard of ideas brings you new ways to look at your world. He may teach you shape shifting, so you can adapt to any environment. He may show you how to turn lead into gold, so you may change good ideas into real moneymakers. He acquires amazing perspective by entering the sacred tree. Use his magic to learn and apply alchemical lessons.

Merlin likes the big picture and can bring much excitement. He can help unlikely pairings of people work together, and get the best out of all of them. He can create genius, where only barrenness had previously dwelt. His counseling ability and wisdom is legendary. When Merlin lands on your doorstep, invite him in and receive a wizard's perspective.

Reversed:

Merlin is very persuasive. He is silver tongued and usually able to get what he wants. If there is anywhere in your life, where you are being 'talked into something', be sure you really need what you are being sold.

Merlin loves big ideas, but can be short on the details. Sometimes, he expects others to do extra work they never anticipated, when they agreed to support his ideas. On the other hand, sometimes charm is a valuable commodity, so be sure and learn the art of rhetoric from the master.

At the very least, hanging around Merlin is really fun and mesmerizing. Keep alert, but enjoy the experience.

Merlin at Stonehenge
from an original drawing
by Mike Heywood

28. Shaman of Water—Sedna

Upright:

Sedna is a goddess of survival When you receive her in a reading, she sees that you have lived through some tough events. They have made you strong. You have transformed difficult emotional lessons, such as betrayal and possibly abuse. You have grown a larger heart and stronger intuition because you now have empathy for other's weaknesses. People you depended on have been vulnerable to their own vices and possibly not there to care for you, when you needed them. You have been able to understand and forgive. You now protect those you love because you never again want to be in the cycle of victimization. In the original story she is not a mermaid, but a battered wife. She is taken by the sea and possibly transformed into a mermaid. Because you have been able to shift emotional pain into love, you too show the skill of transformation, you are acknowledged and blessed by the Shaman of Water.

28. Shaman of Water

Sedna

From an original drawing by DeepGreen
Card design by Don Saunders.

Reversed:

In what way have you been betrayed or neglected? How has someone's selfishness hurt you? Indeed wrong has been done to you. Yet, you will only make your own life harder if you are unable to forgive.

After being neglected, or abused, people often treat themselves the way they were treated by others. There might be self-neglect, addictions, poor eating and sleeping habits. Stop the cycle. You can turn this dysfunctional pattern around, but you must see your worthiness and learn new habits. To do so requires healthy new beliefs and actions that support your new attitudes. Learn to parent yourself in a gentle and loving way. Treat yourself better than others have and grant yourself freedom from the past. Ask yourself if you are 'drying out' in anyway because you are not allowed to be your beautiful, true self? How can you make your life fluid again?

From an original drawing by Fernando Cortes

29. Maven of Water—Kuan Yin

From an original photograph by tanewpix
Card design by Don Saunders.

Upright:

When you get Kuan Yin in a reading compassion is surrounding you. Kuan Yin represents unconditional, non-judgmental love. You are accepted. The Maven of Water is holding you in the highest esteem.

Kuan Yin cares for everyone including: the old, sick, and disgraced. She knows we are all capable of goodness. She sees the beauty and grace you possess. She sees you moving toward a loving way of being, as your future template. The Maven of Water shines adoration and peace in your direction. You are evolving perfectly and Kuan Yin witnesses your progress.

Reversed:

It is time to be kind to yourself and others. If you have not had opportunity to bask in acceptance, now is your opportunity. Kuan Yin sees your potential and grants you forgiveness. Can you now forgive yourself and others? Release the chains of revenge and bitterness and chose a future of compassion.

The light of true kindness and unwavering acceptance is shining on you. Keep your heart open and no matter where you are, the Maven of Water will show the way home.

From an original drawing by Cbenjasuwan

30. Magi of Water—Buddha

From an original drawing by Elenarts
Card design by Don Saunders.

Upright:

When you get Buddha in your reading, you are granted peace and calmness. There is an air of light-hearted joy in your life. There is abundance and emotional stability. You are learning to make sense of the complicated world of emotions. You are staying in the present for longer and longer periods. You see your pain diminishing and in its place is gentle humor and respect for yourself and others.

You see how difficult life and decisions can be. You respect that everyone does his or her best. Your heart is open and you feel love toward all. Oh yes, this is a good day!

Reversed:

Buddha sees that you are trying very hard, but life is still sometimes a struggle. Some situations are indeed difficult. However, all is well.

The Magi of Water reminds you, that wherever you are is perfect. It is in this spot that you are learning how your thoughts and actions create your life. Tomorrow you will be even wiser and able to make even better choices.

When you make decisions that suit who you now are, you create more of what you love. Buddha smiles at you repeatedly. Align yourself increasingly with his peaceful energy.

Bring stillness into your thoughts and tenderness into your actions.

From an original drawing by Elenarts

31. Shaman of Fire—Titania

From an original drawing by olbor62
Card design by Don Saunders.

Upright:

The queen of the fairies has a way of bringing joy when she arrives. She has an ethereal, light and uplifting presence. Titania brings multi-sensory pleasure. She reminds you to walk gently on the earth. Titania works with other nature spirits to keep balance and beauty on Gaia.

Her senses are acute. She helps you get quiet and still. If you listen carefully, she will teach you the song of the wind and the history of the trees. She attunes to the subtle energies of every living being. When the flowers dry out and the water becomes polluted, she hears their cries. She works tirelessly with elemental spirits to meet nature's needs. However, she is here today, to both train you and to get your help. Titania asks if you will be a steward of nature? If you feel her call, attune to the natural elements near you by being still, dreaming their story, and hearing their song. Then use these messages to understand their needs and gently protect them from harm.

Reversed:

Titania brings hope. She is a spirit of brightness and song. She wants you to bathe in the glow of self-love. She asks to see your soft side and for you to treat yourself and those around you with kindness. The world of nature she represents is restorative. She reminds you to spend time in her natural temple to rebalance and heal. Keep a bounce in your footstep and remember to believe in fairies and the magic of your love!

From original drawings by olbor62 and jayteel

32. Maven of Fire—Astarte

Upright:

When Astarte appears she delivers a deep message. She is reminding you of where you originated. You are stardust, part of the star tribe. You came from the same molecules as other, much older beings, in the sky.

Because you are a part of them, they can still reach you and give you their messages. The star tribe is your home.

Astarte brings passion, spirit, and meaning. This Maven of Fire helps you remember what is important in your life.

She points the way to clear seeing and relevant action. Astarte and her priestess, initiate you. She helps you leap into your life confidently.

Astarte can create significant change with one breath. She brings magnificence.

Original artwork by Greg Clark, Arizona
Card design by Don Saunders.

Reversed:

It is easy to feel numb and cut off. If you are feeling alienated from your body and community it is time to come closer to the fire.

Seek out the story of your tribe. Find the people, places and subjects that warm you. Remember the childhood excitement that arose when you thought about what and whom you would be when you grew up.

The Maven of Fire asks "how can you rekindle your inner spark"? Do not waste a day more doing what does not excite you. Your life is happening now, participate and shine brightly. Jump into what brings you joy.

Astarte Syriaca painted by Dante Gabriel Rossetti in 1877

33. Magi of Fire—Bridgid

From an original painting by Paula Pesonen
Card design by Don Saunders.

Upright:

Bridgid carries light, inspiration and illumination into daily tasks. She teaches that the way you live your life is your prayer. She is a bridge between practicality and spirit. The Magi of Fire is a triple goddess, masterful at 'smithing' and the trades. She nudges you to learn useful skills to feel competent and independent. She is also accomplished in poetry, speaking, healing and midwifery. She comes as a mentor in all of these areas. She brings inner healing and fiery vitality. The Magi of Fire is passionate and free. She urges you to look at all of the choices you have that were not open to men and women in her day. She suggests you relish the smorgasbord of opportunity available to you. Create and accomplish, what no one, but you can do. Know every task is your offering and every movement matters.

Reversed:

Take inventory of your functional abilities. What can you add to your repertoire?

Cooking, carpentry, animal husbandry, gardening, wild crafting, canning, welding, and sewing are all useable skills. Having these tools gives you more ways to use your artistic or spiritual abilities. Bridgid wants you to cultivate your whole array of inner resources.

Strengthen yourself physically. Being sedentary and complacent will erode your self-esteem. Bridgid sees the sacredness of spirit and matter and challenges you to build a strong, healthy temple for your body. Recognize how all of your contributions make a difference. Join forces and co-create passion and poetry with the Magi of Fire.

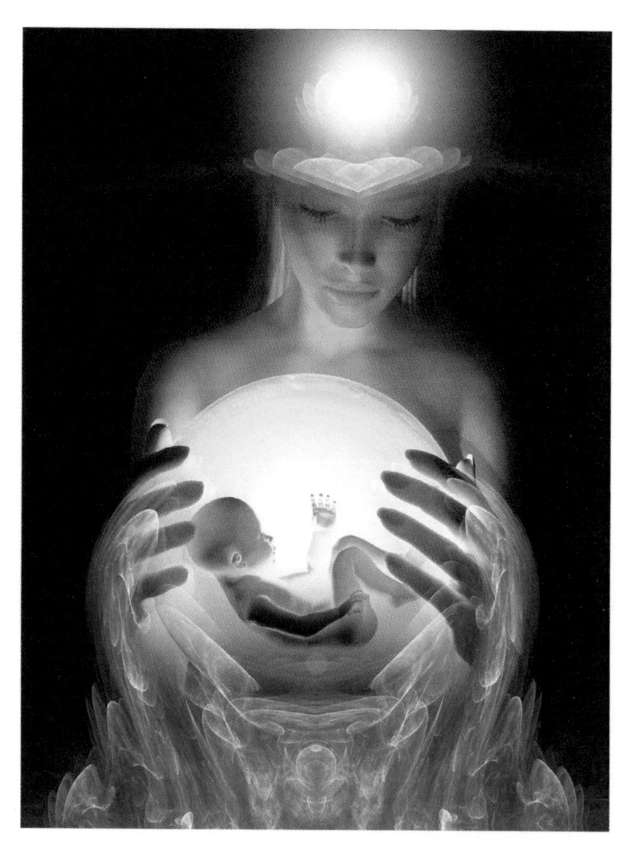

After an original drawing by Desiree Walstra

An original photo illustration by Liliya Kulianionak

An original photo illustration by breaker213

About the Author

Laurie has studied alternative healing since childhood. She is a director of Earth Spirit Medicine and Intuitive Counseling at The Northern Star College of Mystical Studies in Edmonton, Alberta, Canada. www.northernstarcollege.com

Laurie has taught in the Holistic Health Practitioner Program at MacEwan University. Her specialties are aromatherapy, goddesses and mythology, dreamwork, flower essences, and neo-shamanic journeying.

Laurie and her husband Robert are owners of Scents of Wonder, an aromatherapy company, where Laurie has created blends, elixirs and potions for over two decades. Through their company Self Heal Distributing, Laurie and Robert also distribute Prairie Deva Flower Essences of Canada. They are the Canadian Distributors for Healing Herb Essences of England and Californian Essences of the Flower Essence Society, (F.E.S.).

Laurie and Robert live on Mill Creek Ravine, in Edmonton, Alberta, Canada.

Laurie wrote The Path of the Devas in 2006; Healing the Goddess Wound in 2012; The Goddess Wound Workbook, The Healing Goddess Oracle and Scents of Wonder, An Easy Guide to Aromatherapy in 2013, and Scents of Wonder - Aromatic Solutions for Health, Beauty and Pleasure in 2014.

For essential oils, flower essences or copies of this book go to:

www.amazon.com/author/laurieszott-rogers
or
www.selfhealdistributing.com

For courses, try,:

www.northernstarcollege.com

Books by Prairie Deva Press

The Path of the Devas:
Laurie Szott-Rogers
Motivated by his love for Mother Earth, and talent to communicate with plants, Dr. Bo Tannic teaches pre-teens to adults how to connect with nature. He is aided by his colleague Mr. Funguy, an amateur mycologist with a love for food and life and a group of children who find a sense of belonging in their ecological mission. The reader is introduced to a magical cast of characters - the Council of Plants and Nature Devas, as they explore plant medicine and ecology. Join the team as they work to restore a ravine, nurture a forest and stand up to destructive forces.
Fiction, soft cover, 194 pp.

Prairie Deva Flower Essences of the Prairies:
Laurie Szott-Rogers and Robert Rogers
Explore flower essences of the Canadian Prairies, their properties, plant signatures and subtle energy uses.

Healing the Goddess Wound:
Laurie Szott-Rogers
Prairie Deva Press, 2012. 248 pp.
Embark on a journey to meet eight Greek goddesses that enter all women's lives. Each one provides life lessons in a chapter of our psyche's. Each divine being has a different style, intent, influence, and will connect uniquely, with every one of us. On this trip you will discover your goddess soul type, the one with whom you feel most aligned. They arrive as the seasons or cycles of our souls change. If we learn to sense their presence, we can become more conscious while working with them. Having an awareness of 'who is visiting' allows their lessons to flow smoother, and helps our understanding run deeper. For goddess courses visit www.northernstarcollege.com/intuitive

Healing the Goddess Wound Workbook:
Laurie Szott-Rogers, 2013
Go on your own personal retreat with eight Goddesses. Move through their lessons and arrive at your own insights. Do deep, healing inner work as you answer in-depth questions about how you have integrated eight Goddess messages into your own life.
38 pp. Pdf

Scents of Wonder - Aromatic Solutions for Health, Beauty and Pleasure
Laurie Szott-Rogers 2014

Step forward and inhale your own individualized floral paradise. Aromatherapy offers a wide array of scents that keep you smelling the beauty around you, through out your day. Add spearmint to your shower gel to wake you up with zing. Try rosemary in your car diffuser to stay more alert and use chamomile on your pillow to rest more deeply.

Have you ever wanted to create your own spa day? Laurie includes recipes for masks, creams, serums and lotions- inspired by the goddesses, to nourish your skin. Read about the properties of over 100 essential oils, and tips from a 23-year veteran, aromatherapy instructor and blender. This virtual course in aromatherapy offers practical tips to enhance every room of your home. Learn to love what's right under your nose and bring aromatic pleasure into your every day.

Scents of Wonder - An Easy Guide to Aromatherapy:
Laurie Szott-Rogers, 2013
A simple booklet explaining what essential oils are, cautions and how to use them. Twenty top essential oils are discussed. Get to know essential oils and ignite your Scents of Wonder, with this quick and straightforward, aromatic guide.
Approximately 40 pp. Pdf

To learn more, take a moment to visit my author page at:
www.amazon.com/author/laurieszott-rogers

Just some of the many book which have been written by Robert Dale Rogers and which you will find both at www. selfhealdistributing.com and also showcased on his author page which you can find at www.amazon.com/author/robertdalerogers

Oracle Cards

Congratulations! By purchasing this book you are licensed to download a set of printable oracle cards, which have been specially designed and showcased throughout this book.

The cards are contained within a PDF document that should be downloaded and printed out, either on your own home printer, or by taking the PDF file to your local print and copy shop.

Start by downloading the Cards PDF document from:

www.selfhealdistributing.com/ea26-oracle-cards/

Once downloaded, simply open the Cards PDF document. To open the document you will need to enter the following password exactly as it is shown here, using lower case letters for all except the first letter which is an uppercase L.

Lor66cha

Once the document is open, click on the 'File' menu (top left) and then click on 'Print Setup' from the dropdown menu that appears. Make sure that you select the printer attached to your computer and set it to print at a size of US Letter (8.5" x 11") in portrait layout. Once the correct size and orientation is selected, simply click on 'Okay'. Then, click on the 'File' menu again and, this time, select 'Print'. Ensure that 'All pages' is selected and click 'Okay'. Your cards will then print out 4 to a page and the final step will be to cut them into single cards, using scissors or a paper cutter.

For the best results, it is recommended that you print the cards onto a heavy and glossy photographic paper. Please consult the instructions for your printer, or speak to your local dealer, to ascertain the best quality and weight of paper to use with your particular printer. You will need 9 pieces of paper.

Finally, place your cards in a sacred box or bag.

Laurie Szott-Rogers

Made in the USA
Columbia, SC
20 March 2018